The Tortoise Diaries

Daily Meditations

ON CREATIVITY
and
SLOWING DOWN

Christian McEwen

Illustrated by Laetitia Bermejo

BAUHAN PUBLISHING
PETERBOROUGH, NEW HAMPSHIRE
2014

Library of Congress Cataloging-in-Publication Data

The tortoise diaries : daily meditations on creativity and slowing
down / [compiled by] Christian McEwen ; illustrated by Laetitia
Bermejo.
    pages cm
Includes bibliographical references and index.
ISBN 978-0-87233-181-5 (alk. paper)
1. Creation (Literary, artistic, etc.)--Quotations, maxims, etc.
2. Creative ability--Quotations, maxims, etc. 3. Conduct of life-
-Quotations, maxims, etc. 4. Self-actualization (Psychology) I.
McEwen, Christian, 1956- II. Bermejo, Laetitia, illustrator.
PN56.C69T67 2014
801'.92--dc23
                            2014035872

Book designed and typeset
by Henry James and Karina Barriga Albring
Cover Design by Henry James
Cover Painting by Laetitia Bermejo

BAUHAN
PUBLISHING LLC
PO BOX 117 PETERBOROUGH NEW HAMPSHIRE 03458
                        603-567-4430
WWW.BAUHANPUBLISHING.COM

PRINTED IN THE UNITED STATES OF AMERICA

For Tish,
with love and gratitude

Slowly, slowly—

We called him Tortoise because he taught us.

-LEWIS CARROLL

Introduction

In the fall of 2011, I published a book called
*World Enough & Time: On Creativity and Slowing
Down*. It could be read from start to finish,
like any regular book. But because it was
composed of 115 short sections, it could
also be used as a source of daily prayer or
meditation, focusing on one short portion
at a time. In other words, it could serve to
practice *lectio divina* or "divine reading." As
time went on, I was delighted to learn that it
was indeed being used in just this way.
However, the book itself is fairly bulky,
and several friends suggested that a more
compact version would be welcome: a diary
perhaps, or daily reader. This was the origin

of *The Tortoise Diaries*: a mini treasure-house of poems and quotations, centered, like the original text, on creativity and slowing down.

Because *World Enough & Time* contained twelve chapters, and there are twelve months to every year, it seemed natural to transfer the structure from one book to the other, focusing in turn on different subjects, so that the month of January is used to introduce "the art of slowing down," February to consider good company and conversation, March to investigate "child time," and April, the joys and relaxation to be found in walking. Those who are familiar with the original text will recognize many of the entries, which have been arranged so as to flow smoothly from one to the next, helping to deepen and clarify each particular theme.

The title is drawn, with laughing gratitude, from Lewis Carroll ("We called him Tortoise because he taught us.") though it has more ancient origins too. In Hindu mythology, the world is supported on the back of a gigantic tortoise; a belief also found in many Native American traditions. The tortoise may be slow, but it is sturdy and self-sufficient. Its lineage extends back some 230 million years, likely predating both birds and mammals, even dinosaurs. It is immensely long-lived. Not surprisingly, it represents many stalwart virtues, from fertility and regeneration, to strength and longevity and eternal life. It is associated with art and creativity too; the Greeks believed that the first musical instrument (the lyre) was made by Hermes from an empty tortoiseshell.

And of course the tortoise, "slow and steady," is the one who wins the race.

CHRISTIAN MCEWEN

January

January 1

The minute rages in the clock.

—THEODORE ROETHKE

January 2

For fast-acting relief from stress, try
slowing down.

—LILY TOMLIN

January 3

It is in our idleness, in our dreams, that the submerged truth sometimes comes to the top.

—VIRGINIA WOOLF

January 4

The frenzy of the activist neutralizes his work for peace.

—THOMAS MERTON

January 5

Our senses are currently whip-driven
by a feverish new pace of technological
change. The activities that mark us as
human, though, don't begin, exist in, or
end by such a calculus. They pulse, fade
out, and pulse again in human tissue,
human nerves, and in the elemental
humus of memory, dreams, and art,
where there are no bygone eras. They are
in us . . . they can teach us if we desire it.

—ADRIENNE RICH

January 6

Art is the means we have of undoing the damage of haste. It's what everything else isn't.

—THEODORE ROETHKE

January 7

More and more I find I want to be living
in a Big Here and a Long Now.

—BRIAN ENO

January 8

There is a thread you follow. It goes among things that change. But it doesn't change. People wonder about what you are pursuing. You have to explain about the thread.

—WILLIAM STAFFORD

January 9

Beware the barrenness of a busy life.

—SOCRATES

January 10

A broad margin of leisure is as beautiful in a man's life as in a book.

—HENRY DAVID THOREAU

January 11

There is more to life than merely increasing its speed.

—MOHANDAS GANDHI

January 12

We take for granted the appeal of velocity, that there is money to be made and pleasure to be had from the gratification of the instantaneous: the three-gulp Happy Meal, the lightning download, the vital mobile phone message that I am here and are you there? And where has this culture of haste got us?

—SIMON SCHAMA

January 13

Idleness is often empowering,
recreating oneself—
just as the moon gradually
grows full once again
. . .
so everything, everyone
must have time for the self—
for mirth and laziness
time to be human.

—DORIS KAREVA
translated from the Estonian by Tina Aleman

Millions of Americans have lost control of the basic rhythm of their daily lives. They work too much, eat too quickly, socialize too little, drive and sit in traffic for too many hours, don't get enough sleep, and feel harried too much of the time.

—JULIET SCHOR

January 15

I want to say, in all seriousness, that a great deal of harm is being done in the modern world by belief in the virtuousness of work, and the road to happiness and prosperity lies in an organized diminution of work.

—BERTRAND RUSSELL

January 16

What was lost? Time varied, elastic and colored. Time local, mischievous and ribboned. Time seasonal, haphazard, red-lettered and unpredictable was gone. Time was . . . colonized. Mapped. Leveled. Privatized. Enclosed. Counted in and accounted out.

—JAY GRIFFITHS

January 17

Slow down, our sages advise, slow down all the way to the pace of stone and shadow.

—DIANE ACKERMAN

January 18

Space is the twin sister of time. If we have open space then we have open time to breathe, to dream, to dare, to play, to pray, to move freely, in a world our minds have forgotten, but our bodies remember. Time and space. This partnership is holy.

—TERRY TEMPEST WILLIAMS

January 19

While washing the dishes one should only be washing the dishes, which means that while washing the dishes one should be completely aware of the fact that one is washing the dishes. At first glance, that might seem a little silly: why put so much stress on a simple thing? But that's precisely the point.

—THICH NHAT HANH

January 20

Perpetual devotion to what a man calls his business, is only to be sustained by perpetual neglect of many other things. . . . Look at one of your industrious fellows. . . . He sows hurry and reaps indigestion.

—ROBERT LOUIS STEVENSON

January 21

To see how much I can get done in a day
does not impress me any more.

—TERRY TEMPEST WILLIAMS

January 22

Life is so short, we must move very slowly.

—THAI PROVERB

January 23

Work hard, be lazy.

—NAM JUNE PAIK

January 24

Everybody gets so much information all day long that they lose their common sense.

—GERTRUDE STEIN

January 25

To let body, soul and mind become tranquil is not idleness; it is work of the most difficult kind; it means directing oneself (through discipline) toward real life.

—KARLFRIED DÜRCKHEIM

January 26

Be out of sync with your times for just
one day, and you will see how much
eternity you contain within you.

—RAINER MARIA RILKE

January 27

Culture, as I understand it, is essentially the product of leisure. The art of culture is, essentially, the art of loafing . . . . The wisest man is therefore he who loafs most gracefully.

—LIN YUTANG

January 28

After lighting a lamp, I took out my pen and ink, and closed my eyes, trying to remember the sights I had seen and the poems I had composed during the day.

—BASHO

January 29

It is not that we have so little time, but that we waste so much of it.

—SENECA

January 30

The soul has its own sense of time, and its own odd forms of clock and calendar. Some days are long, some short.

—STEPHAN RECHTSCHAFFEN

January 31

Who are we? That is the first question. It is a question almost impossible to answer. But we all agree that the busy self occupied in our daily activities is not quite the real self. We are quite sure we have lost something in the mere pursuit of living.

—LIN YUTANG

February

February 1

The ear draws forth the story.

—ITALO CALVINO

February 2

I'd like you to see how differently we're all moving, how the time allowed to let things become known grows shorter and shorter, how quickly things and people get replaced.

—ADRIENNE RICH

February 3

Things are in the saddle, and ride mankind.

—RALPH WALDO EMERSON

February 4

Seek society. Keep your friendships in repair. Answer your letters, Meet goodwill half-way.

—RALPH WALDO EMERSON

February 5

A man has as many friends as he has personalities within him.

—PAUL VALÉRY

February 6

The bird a nest, the spider a web, man friendship.

—WILLIAM BLAKE

February 7

I was the first one to start a café on the block. Now they're calling the neighborhood Little Egypt. . . . What we do, we make the area nice. We don't have much, so we create a state of mind to enjoy ourselves. . . . We get together and talk about literature and art.

—ALI EL SAYED

February 8

Among the different kinds of friends,
those who can write poems are
best, those who can talk or hold a
conversation come second, those who
can paint come next, those who can
sing come fourth, and those who can
understand wine games come last.

—LIN YUTANG

February 9

A humble friend in the same village is better than sixteen influential brothers in the Royal Palace.

—CHINESE PROVERB

February 10

Sincere and happy conversation doubles our power. In the effort to unfold our thought to a friend, we make it clearer to ourselves.

—RALPH WALDO EMERSON

February 11

I loved to listen to her talk. I was never happier than on the nights we stayed home, lying on the living room rug. We talked about classes and poetry and politics and sex . . . . Iowa City in the eighties was never going to be Paris in the twenties, but we gave it our best shot.

—ANN PATCHETT

February 12

[Humboldt] was always accompanied
by a swarm, a huge volume of notions.
. . . To talk to him was sustaining,
nourishing.

—SAUL BELLOW

In those two Miles he broached a
thousand things . . . —Nightingales,
Poetry—on Poetical sensation—
Metaphysics—Different genera and
species of Dreams—Nightmare—a
dream accompanied with a sense of
touch . . . —a dream related—First and
second consciousness—the difference
explained between will and Volition . . .
—Monsters—the Kraken—Mermaids—
Southey believes in them—Southey's
belief too much diluted—a Ghost story—

—JOHN KEATS

of Samuel Taylor Coleridge's conversation

February 14

When we do find a true conversationalist, the pleasure is equal to, if not above, that of reading a delightful author, with the additional pleasure of hearing his voice and seeing his gestures. Sometimes we find it at the happy reunion of old friends, . . . sometimes in the smoking room of a night train, and sometimes at an inn on a distant journey.

—LIN YUTANG

February 15

What happens if you make a distinction between what you tell your friends and what you tell your Muse? The problem is to break down that distinction: when you approach your Muse to talk as frankly as you would talk with yourself or with your friends.

—ALLEN GINSBERG

February 16

Real conversation has an unpredictability, danger, and resonance; it can take a turn anywhere and constantly borders on the unexpected and on the unknown.

—JOHN O'DONOHUE

February 17

At our very first meeting, we talked with
continually increasing intimacy. We
seemed to sink though layer after layer
of what was superficial till gradually
both reached the central fire. It was
an experience unlike any other I have
known. We looked into each other's eyes
half appalled and half intoxicated to find
ourselves together in such a region.

—BERTRAND RUSSELL
on his friendship with Joseph Conrad

February 18

John Wesley's conversation is good,
but he is never at leisure. He is always
obliged to go at a certain hour. This is
very disagreeable to a man who loves to
fold his legs and have out his talk, as I do.

—SAMUEL JOHNSON

February 19

Busyness is our art form, our civic ritual, our way of being us.

—ADAM GOPNIK

February 20

One of the first lessons for the talker is
to learn the art of listening.

—STEPHEN MILLER

February 21

A dear Room with such dear Friends, &
such a dear Fire, that I seemed to love
the moving Shadows on the wall, for
their own sake. . .

—SAMUEL TAYLOR COLERIDGE

February 22

An evening spent with friends can measurably enhance the immune system for two days.

—MARK SLOUKA

Oh, the comfort—the inexpressible comfort of feeling safe with a person, having neither to weigh thoughts nor measure words, but pouring them all right out, just as they are, chaff and grain together, certain that a faithful hand will take and sift them, keep what is worth keeping and then with a breath of kindness blow the rest away.

—GEORGE ELIOT

February 24

Let us draw closer to the fire so that we may better see what we are saying.

—CHINESE SAYING

February 25

He listened. He did not just politely
pretend to listen, while impatiently
waiting for her to finish what she was
saying and shut up. . . . He was in no
hurry, and he never rushed her. He
would wait for her to finish. . . .

—AMOS OZ

February 26

I was fascinated by the way Buber
spoke. . . . He took time between
utterances, time to pause, to listen.
For Buber, speaking was a way of
listening.

—MICHAEL EIGEN

February 27

When we no longer hear the warbler
and the wren, our own speaking can no
longer be nourished by their cadences.

—DAVID ABRAM

February 28

The rain surrounded the cabin . . . with a whole world of meaning, of secrecy, of rumor . . . . . It will talk as long as it wants, the rain. As long as it talks, I am going to listen.

—THOMAS MERTON

February 29

Some people go to priests; others to
poetry; I to my friends.

—VIRGINA WOOLF

March

March 1

Tomorrow, will we have hundreds of times to play?

—GEORGIA MCEWEN

aged 4

March 2

Once in a sycamore I was glad / all at the top, and I sang.

—JOHN BERRYMAN

March 3

If I belonged to anything, it was to the small, but then enormous, landscapes of my childhood, to houses, trees, gardens, walks—only then was my absorption so utter that I felt no separation between myself and an outside world.

—ALASTAIR REID

March 4

All children want to crouch in their
secret nests.

—SEAMUS HEANEY

March 5

There was a child went forth every day,
And the first object he look'd upon,
that object he became.

—WALT WHITMAN

March 6

To learn from a pine things about a pine, and from a bamboo things about a bamboo.

—BASHO

Two blocks from home the human world
dwindled to a path threading through
nettle and alder. A spider web across
the path meant no one was there before
me. I crawled under its fragile gate to
solitude and was gone.

—KIM STAFFORD

March 8

The childhood landscape is learned on foot, and a map is inscribed in the mind—trails and pathways and groves—the mean dog, the cranky old man's house, the pasture with a bull in it—going out wider and farther . . . . You can almost totally recall the place you walked, played, biked, swam.

—GARY SNYDER

March 9

Most people seem to have a ditch somewhere . . . [or a creek or a meadow, a woodlot or marsh]. . . . these are places of initiation, where the borders between ourselves and other creatures break down, where the earth gets under our nails and a sense of place gets under our skin.

—ROBERT MICHAEL PYLE

March 10

That was the main thing about kids
then: we spent an awful lot of time
doing nothing. . . . picking wild
flowers. Catching tadpoles. Looking
for arrowheads. Getting our feet wet.
Playing with mud. And sand. And water.
You understand, not doing anything.

—ROBERT PAUL SMITH

The star-filled sky, meadows in bloom,
tumbling rivers, soaring raven songs—
all of these are needed to shape the spirit
of the child.

—THOMAS BERRY

March 12

There is a sacred otherness to the world
that is breathtakingly helpful.

—DAVID WHYTE

March 13

I begin two years of glorious illiteracy—a
period, I subsequently realize, of which
I have almost total recall: for the world
around me is my only book. I learn about
herbs and herbal medicine, plant myths,
river myths, thievery. . .

—PADMA HEJMADI

March 14

Little did I know what my children would
allow me to see: Lilliputian landscapes
often overlooked by educated adults
seeking the Big Picture.

—GARY PAUL NABHAN

March 15

My life changed abruptly when I started
school . . . . Now, when I woke up I
checked the clock a million times, both
the alarm clock on the night table and
the huge clock on the street corner just
opposite my window. I hated those two
clocks. My life was gradually being taken
over by things I hated.

—NATALIA GINZBURG

March 16

I remember the desperate desire to cling
to the last moments before time had
ticked them away . . . . I used to stand
on the beach and look around and say to
myself: "I'm here now, *at this minute*, and
nothing can take this minute away." But
it went.

—DAVID DAICHES

March 17

You must empty your pockets, turn them inside out, and spill out your wife and your son, the pets you hardly knew, and the days you simply missed altogether watching the sunlight fade on the bricks across the way. You must hand over the rainy afternoons, the light on the grass, the moments of play and of simply being. You must give it up, all of it, and by your example teach your children to do the same.

—MARK SLOUKA

March 18

Nobody running at full speed has either
a head or a heart.

—W.B. YEATS

March 19

You cannot put a child in front of a television set where he is bombarded by images and not ultimately have an adult who is born and bred to see things differently.

—JAMES GLEIK

March 20

People never seemed to notice that, by saving time, they were losing something else. No one cared to admit that life was becoming ever poorer, bleaker and more monotonous. The ones who felt this most keenly were the children, because no one had time for them anymore.

—MICHAEL ENDE

March 21

Most children have a bug period, and I never outgrew mine. . . . Better to be an untutored savage for a while, not to know the names or anatomical detail. Better to spend long stretches of time just searching and dreaming.

—E.O. WILSON

March 22

There's no clock in the forest.

—WILLIAM SHAKESPEARE

March 23

I am quite sure that amidst the hustle
and bustle of American life, there is a
great deal of wistfulness, of the divine
desire to lie on a plot of grass under tall
beautiful trees of an idle afternoon and
just do nothing.

—LIN YUTANG

March 24

The tree which moves some to tears of joy is in the Eyes of others only a Green thing which stands in the way.

—WILLIAM BLAKE

March 25

You are yourself a sequoia. . . . Stop and
get acquainted with your big brethren.

—JOHN MUIR
to Ralph Waldo Emerson

March 26

I sit for a long time and watch one thing. If you don't do that homework, you don't make yourself vulnerable enough to a place, and it never releases itself into you.

—BARRY LOPEZ

March 27

To the digital generation, I suppose time is linear. The minutes fall away, never to be heard from again. There is no record of the past and no promise of the future, only the swiftly vanishing present.

—NANCY WILLARD

March 28

Downtime is when we become ourselves,
looking into the middle distance,
kicking at the curb, lying on the grass
or sitting on the stoop and staring at the
tedious blue of the summer sky. I don't
believe you can write poetry or compose
music, or become an actor without
downtime and plenty of it. A hiatus
that passes for boredom is really the
quiet moving of wheels inside that fuel
creativity.

—ANNA QUINDLEN

March 29

Mercifully, I had time to imagine, fantasize, play with paper dolls and china figurines, inventing and resolving their fates. The best times were times I was ignored, could talk stories under my breath, loving my improvised world almost as much as I loved reading.

—ADRIENNE RICH

March 30

When I played with boys as a child,
we rode horses, we played cowboys
and Indians or rustlers: the land was
backdrop. When I played with girls, the
land and animals were central; we didn't
just ride horses, we *became* them.

—THERESA JORDAN

March 31

One of the very best things about the world is that so little of it is me.

—ANDREW GREIG

April

April 1

Why has the pleasure of slowness disappeared? Ah, where have they gone, the amblers of yesteryear? Where have they gone, those loafing heroes of folk song, those vagabonds who roam from one mill to another and bed down under the stars?

—MILAN KUNDERA

April 2

The trouble with the rat race is that even if you win, you're still a rat.

—LILY TOMLIN

April 3

Now, here, you see, it takes all the running you can do to keep in the same place. If you want to get somewhere else, you must run at least twice as fast as that!

—LEWIS CARROLL

April 4

I can't even enjoy a blade of grass unless
I know there's a subway handy.

—FRANK O'HARA

April 5

The true motive of travel should be to become lost and unknown.

—LIN YUTANG

Consider this utterly commonplace situation: a man walking down the street. At a certain moment he tries to recall something, but the recollection escapes him. Automatically, he slows down.

—MILAN KUNDERA

April 7

I was in my tent one night and just listening to the rain, and wondering, you know, why I was there. And what was it about? So, it was a good time for reflection. And one thing that came to me was that I just like moving myself about by my own speed.

—PARKER HUBER

April 8

Walking takes longer . . . than any other known form of locomotion except crawling. Thus, it stretches time and prolongs life. . . . Walking makes the world much bigger and therefore more interesting. You have time to observe the details.

—EDWARD ABBEY

April 9

The mind is also a landscape of sorts,
and . . . walking is one way to traverse it.

—REBECCA SOLNIT

April 10

My walks were almost daily on the top of the Quantock, and among its sloping coombs. With my pencil and memorandum book in my hand, I was making *studies*, as the artists call them, and often moulding my thoughts into verse, with the objects and imagery immediately before my senses.

—SAMUEL TAYLOR COLERIDGE

April 11

In my room, the world is beyond my understanding;
But when I walk I see that it consists of three or four hills and a cloud.

—WALLACE STEVENS

Poetry refers by its every formal wile
to our urge to go slower, and that
longing is part of poetry's authority for
heartbreak. Travel is like that. You walk
for a while. You stand there and sip. You
stand there and look.

—WILLIAM MATTHEWS

April 13

Chance furnishes me what I need. I am like a man who stumbles along; my foot strikes something. I bend over, and it is exactly what I want.

—JAMES JOYCE

April 14

Few men know how to take a walk. The qualifications . . . are endurance, plain clothes, old shoes, an eye for Nature, good humor, vast curiosity, good speech, good silence and nothing too much.

—RALPH WALDO EMERSON

April 15

Tonight, after leaving the Hospital, at
10 o'clock, (I had been on self-imposed
duty some five hours, pretty closely
confined,) I wander'd a long time
around Washington. The night was
sweet, very clear, sufficiently cool, a
voluptuous half-moon slightly golden,
the space near it of a transparent tinge.
. . . I wander'd to and fro till the moist
moon set, long after midnight.

—WALT WHITMAN

April 16

He walked in a very relaxed way, and when he sat down he would remain in balance. He was never in a hurry . . . . He always took the time to do everything. That's being in time.

—DAVID CHADWICK
of Shunryu Suzuki

April 17

I dropped my watch into the stream of time.

—THEODORE ROETHKE

April 18

A snowstorm in the morning, and
continuing most of the day. But I took
a walk over two hours, the same woods
and paths, amid the falling flakes. No
wind, yet the musical low murmur
through the pines, quite pronounced,
curious, like waterfalls, now still'd, now
pouring again. All the senses, sight,
sound, smell, delicately gratified.

—WALT WHITMAN

April 19

It was a pleasure and a privilege to walk with him. He knew the country like a fox or a bird, and passed through it as freely by paths of his own. He knew every track in the snow or on the ground, and what creature had taken his path before him.

—RALPH WALDO EMERSON
of Henry David Thoreau

April 20

Above all, do not lose your desire to walk. Every day I walk myself into a state of well-being and walk away from every illness that would have me; I have walked myself into my best thoughts, and I know of no thought so burdensome that one cannot walk away from it.

—SØREN KIERKEGAARD

April 21

Solvitur ambulando: you can sort it out by walking.

—LATIN PROVERB

April 22

I'm much taken these days with feral
walking. I make no plans, except to
begin and end in the same place and
follow as few made paths as possible.
Instead I tag along on deer trails, head
for trees on the horizon, give in to the
slightest instinct to change tracks, and
hope I'm being guided by cues below the
level of my conscious attention.

—RICHARD MABEY

April 23

A morning walk to the mailbox. True
I should have "saved" about twenty-
five minutes of my priceless time. For
what? For the sake of a more sluggish
digestion, of a wider girth beneath
my belt, staler air in my lungs, duller
thoughts in my head, a posture grown
that much older, I should have lopped
off half an hour of fresh and living
experience.

—DONALD CULROSS PEATTIE

I am a hunter, I take the opportunities each day offers—if it is snowing, I work with snow, at leaf-fall it will be with leaves, a blown-over tree becomes a source of twigs and branches. I stop at a place or pile up a material by feeling that there is something to be discovered. . . . There are places I return to over and over again, going deeper.

—ANDY GOLDSWORTHY

April 25

Do not walk so fast, the rain is everywhere.

—SHUNRYU SUZUKI

April 26

Not to keep hours for a lifetime is, I was going to say, to live forever. You have no idea, unless you have tried it, how endlessly long is a summer's day.

—ROBERT LOUIS STEVENSON

I only went out for a walk, and finally concluded to stay out till sundown; for going out, I found, was really going in.

—JOHN MUIR

April 28

Artists and poets have a responsibility
to the landscape, to wild nature. . . .
not copying the landscape, but finally
becoming the landscape.

—NANAO SAKAKI

April 29

What I write begins and ends with the act of noticing and cherishing, and it neither begins nor ends with the human world. . . . I am forever just going out for a walk and tripping over the root, or the petal, of some trivia, then seeing it as if in a second sight, as emblematic.

—MARY OLIVER

April 30

Early one morning, any morning, we can set out, with the least possible baggage, and discover the world.

—THOMAS A. CLARK

May

May 1

Stare. Educate the eye.
Die knowing something.
You are not here long.

—WALKER EVANS

May 2

Nobody sees a flower, really—it is so small—we haven't time, and to see takes time.

—GEORGIA O' KEEFFE

May 3

Every year, the time most of us spend actually *seeing* our world—actual men's and women's bodies rather than models in advertisements, actual landscapes rather than images of landscapes on television—grows smaller.

—MARK SLOUKA

May 4

My home stands on a wooded bench, set back about two hundred feet from the north bank of the McKenzie River in western Oregon. Almost every day I go down to the river with no intention but to sit and watch. I have been watching the river for thirty years . . . . If I have learned anything here, it's that each time I come down, something I don't know yet will reveal itself.

—BARRY LOPEZ

May 5

I must walk with more free senses—
. . . . It is as bad to *study* stars & clouds
as flowers & stones—I must let my
senses wander as my thoughts—my eyes
see without looking. . . . What I need is
not to look at all—but a true sauntering
of the eye.

—HENRY DAVID THOREAU

May 6

I have no news to tell you, for the days are all the same, I have no ideas, except to think that a field of wheat or a cypress is well worth the trouble of looking at close up, and so on.

—VINCENT VAN GOGH

May 7

One day I discovered an entirely new joy. Suddenly, at the age of forty, I began to paint. . . . Painting is marvelous; it makes one happier and more patient. Afterward one does not have black fingers as with writing, but red and blue ones.

—HERMANN HESSE

May 8

Just looking alone has no grit in it . . . .
That only happens while you are
drawing.

—HENRY MOORE

May 9

A line comes into being. . . . It goes out
for a walk, so to speak, aimlessly for the
sake of the walk.

—PAUL KLEE

May 10

I wanted to draw a dog. I sat beside
Carlow's kennel and stared at him a long
time. Then I took a charred stick from
the grate, split open a large brown-paper
sack and drew a dog on the sack. . . . The
paper sack was found years later among
Father's papers. He had written on it,
"By Emily, aged eight."

—EMILY CARR

May 11

From the age of six I had a mania for drawing the form of things. By the time I was fifty I had published an infinity of designs: but all that I have produced before the age of seventy is not worth taking into account. At seventy-three, I have learned a little about the real structure of nature, of animals, plants, birds, fishes, and insects. . . . when I am a hundred and ten, everything I do, be it but a dot or a line, will be alive.

—HOKUSAI

May 12

I believe that the sight is a more important thing than the drawing; and I would rather teach drawing that my pupils may learn to love Nature, than teach the looking at nature that they may learn to draw.

—JOHN RUSKIN

May 13

When you go outside to draw you're not walking, you're not hiking, you're not talking, you're just sitting. Just through the physics of the act, you're somewhat still. Out of this quiet, the world starts to emerge. The birds are curious and come closer. . . . [You] begin to hear and see in a different way.

—BARBARA BASH

May 14

I have learned that what I have not drawn
I have never really seen, and that when I
start drawing an ordinary thing I realize
how extraordinary it is, sheer miracle.

—FREDERICK FRANCK

May 15

Drawing itself is a part of learning:
learning to use one's eyes more
intensely.

—HENRY MOORE

May 16

I myself have never made a dead set at studying Nature with notebook and field glass in hand. I have rather visited with her. We have walked together or sat down together, and our intimacy grows with the seasons.

—JOHN BURROUGHS

May 17

To see a wren in a bush, call it "wren" and go on walking is to have . . . seen nothing. To see a bird and stop, watch, feel, forget yourself for a moment, be in the bushy shadows, maybe then feel "wren"—that is to have joined in a larger moment with the world

—GARY SNYDER

May 18

I remember walking to school as a little boy, amazed at all the things I'd never noticed. . . . For some reason, the discovery of this hidden world, a world that was mine for the looking, made me enormously happy.

—SAM SWOPE

May 19

The true voyage of discovery consists not in seeking new landscapes, but in having new eyes.

—MARCEL PROUST

May 20

Being an artist means: not numbering and counting, but ripening like a tree, which doesn't force its sap, and stands confidently in the storms of spring, not afraid that afterward summer may not come. It does come but it comes only to those who are patient, who are there as if eternity lay before them, so unconcernedly silent and vast.

—RAINER MARIA RILKE

May 21

. . . it is our slowness I love, growing slower,
tapping the paintbrush against the visible,
tapping the mind.

—JORIE GRAHAM

May 22

[In the days before photography] A painter might only see a rare painting once, for a few minutes, and then it would have to be held in memory for years, and perhaps for an entire lifetime.

—JAMES ELKINS

May 23

I have never enjoyed to the utmost a
work of art of any kind, whether verbal,
musical or visual, never enjoyed a
landscape, without sinking my identity
into that work of art, without becoming
it.

—BERNARD BERENSON

May 24

Art does not reproduce the visible, but makes visible.

—PAUL KLEE

May 25

Many years ago I went to a museum with my father. I was looking at a painting for a long time—it was by Paul Klee—and my father said, "Do you know what most people are thinking when they're looking? They're thinking, 'That's nice. What time is lunch?'"

—ESTHER COHEN

May 26

Gradually a great delight filled me, dispelling all boredom and doubts about what I ought to like. . . . Yet it had all happened by just sitting still and waiting. If I had merely given a cursory glance, said, "Isn't that a nice Cézanne," and drifted on with the crowd, I would have missed it all.

—MARION MILNER

May 27

Modern art spreads joy around by its color, which calms us.

—HENRY MATISSE

May 28

The greatest thing a human being ever does in this world is to SEE something, and tell what he saw in a plain way. Hundreds of people can talk for one who can think, but thousands of people can think for one who can see. To see clearly is poetry, prophecy and religion—all in one.

—JOHN RUSKIN

May 29

It's like a firework: well, no, it's really like a Persian rug. Are all these millions of little branches really so wonderfully wrought? Just look at the radiance of this green which contains a little gold, and the sandalwood warmth of the brown in the little stems, and that fissure with its new, fresh, inner barely-green.

—RAINER MARIA RILKE
looking closely at a sprig of heather

May 30

Smoky corn and wild rose, faded roses
(3 reds), nuts and nettles faded roses and
vermilion roses in a yellow basket. . . .
cyclamen and straw and earth.

—GWEN JOHN'S PAINTING NOTES

May 31

Suddenly one has the right eyes.

—RAINER MARIA RILKE

June

June 1

Only one hour of the normal day is more pleasurable than the hour spent in bed with a book before going to sleep and that is the hour spent in bed with a book after being called in the morning.

—RAINER MARIA RILKE

June 2

Any work of art makes one very simple demand on anyone who genuinely wants to get in touch with it. And that is to stop. You've got to stop what you're doing, what you're thinking, and what you're expecting and just be there for the poem for however long it takes.

—W.S. MERWIN

June 3

Poetry is about slowing down . . . it's about reading the same thing again and again, really savoring it, living inside the poem.

—MARK STRAND

June 4

I have an idea that a Man might pass a very pleasant life in this manner – let him on any certain day read a certain Page of full Poesy or distilled Prose and let him wander with it, and muse upon it, and reflect from it, and bring home to it, and prophesy upon it, and dream upon it. . . . How happy is such a "voyage of conception," what delicious diligent Indolence!

—JOHN KEATS

The average book fits into the human hand with a seductive nestling, a kiss of texture, whether of cover cloth, glazed jacket, or flexible paperback.

—JOHN UPDIKE

June 6

Men are made by books.

—THEODORE ROETHKE

June 7

To read a story well is to follow it, to act it, to feel it, to become it.

—URSULA LE GUIN

June 8

Try opening your favorite books and reading the endings aloud. Chances are you'll find yourself reading more slowly, and perhaps more softly, as the sentences themselves telegraph the arrival of a grand or muted finale.

—FRANCINE PROSE

June 9

When I'm reading Hopkins aloud, I feel
I am actually occupying his selfhood and
speaking out of it, not simply reciting
the words, but somehow merging into
his bloodstream and nervous system.

—STANLEY KUNITZ

While most prose is a kind of continuous chatter, describing, naming, explaining, poetry speaks against an essential backdrop of silence. . . . There is a prayerful, haunted silence between words, between phrases, between images, ideas, and lines. This is one reason why good poems can be read over and over. The reader, perhaps without knowing it, instinctively desires to peer between the cracks into the other world where the unspoken rests in darkness.

—JAMES TATE

June 11

Herman has taken to writing poetry. You need not tell anyone, for you know how such things get around.

—MRS. MELVILLE
writing to her mother

June 12

Sometimes the world loses its face. It becomes too base. The task of the poet is to restore its face, because otherwise man is lost in doubt and despair.

—CZESLAW MILOSZ

June 13

This is, therefore, the intensest
rendezvous.

—WALLACE STEVENS

June 14

There is then creative reading as well as creative writing.

—RALPH WALDO EMERSON

June 15

Books gleamed from the walls,
beautifully bound or carefully jacketed
in paper, for he liked books as he liked
dumb animals.

—STEPHAN ZWEIG
of Rainer Maria Rilke

June 16

The public library was the best place
in town. Incredibly, they'd let you take
those thick art books home so you could
sit in your kitchen, eat your hot dogs and
beans, and study the paintings of Giotto
and Rembrandt. . . . I read riding to
work; I read while pretending to shuffle
papers on my desk; I read in bed and fell
asleep with the lights still on.

—CHARLES SIMIC

June 17

There is such a thing as an affinity of spirits, and among the authors of ancient and modern times, one must try to find an author whose spirit is akin to his own. . . . Who is one's favorite author, no one can tell, probably not even the man himself. It is like love at first sight.

—LIN YUTANG

June 18

I have often thought that we were meant for each other—you to write to me and I to read you . . . every sentence I have ever read of yours gave me immediate intense pleasure—at the world as you saw it, and at how you said what you were saying . . . . That influence has long since gone into my bones.

—WILLIAM MAXWELL
to Sylvia Townsend Warner

June 19

When the landscape buckles and jerks
around, when a dust column of debris
rises from the collapse of a block of
buildings on bodies that could have been
your own, when the staves of history fall
awry and the barrel of time bursts apart,
some turn to prayer, some to poetry:
words in the memory, a stained book
carried close to the body, the notebook
scribbled by hand—a center of gravity.

—ADRIENNE RICH

June 20

What use is poetry?

I sat down September twelfth,
two thousand-one in the Common
   Era
and read Rumi and kissed the
ground.

—SAM HAMILL

June 21

[This] country is proud of its dead poets.
It takes terrific satisfaction in the poet's
testimony that the USA is too tough,
too big, too much, too rugged, that
American reality is overpowering. And to
be a poet is a school thing, a skirt thing,
a church thing.

—SAUL BELLOW

June 22

The shelf life of the average trade book is somewhere between milk and yogurt.

—CALVIN TRILLIN

June 23

What made Wordsworth's poems a medicine for my state of mind, was that they expressed, not mere outward beauty, but states of feeling, and of thought colored by feeling, under the excitement of beauty. . . . In them I seemed to draw from a source of inward joy, of sympathetic and imaginative pleasure, which could be shared in by all human beings.

—JOHN STUART MILL

June 24

My grandfather taught me that when you are sick, you should take a bowl of water and you should read to it. If you know the Koran, read the Koran. But it doesn't really matter what you read, so long as it is something that has real meaning to you. Then you take the water and wash yourself with it, and you will get well.

—SAUDI STORY

June 25

Poetry can repair no loss, but it defies
the space which separates. And it
does this by its continual labour of
reassembling what has been scattered.

—JOHN BERGER

June 26

To read a book of poetry
from back to front,
there is the cure for certain kinds of
    sadness.

A person only has to choose.
What doesn't matter; just that—

—JANE HIRSHFIELD

June 27

I loved especially the *sounds* of words.
We were fortunate in our house to have
an unabridged dictionary. I explored it
every day for new words and I would go
out into the woods behind our house
and shout my latest discovery and listen
to it reverberate. I considered it my duty
to give my new words to the elements, to
scatter them.

—STANLEY KUNITZ

June 28

Every book is worth reading which puts the reader in a working mood.

—RALPH WALDO EMERSON

June 29

It's funny, you read someone like T. H. White for an hour in the early morning, and your mind grooves on him and your find yourself writing away downhill as if guided and balanced by his invisible hand at your elbow. You don't have to even think about a thing. Just push off and freewheel.

—ROGER DEAKIN

June 30

Reading books in one's youth is like looking at the moon through a crevice; reading books in middle age is like looking at the moon in one's courtyard; and reading books in old age is like looking at the moon on an open terrace.

—CHANG CH'AO

July

July 1

A writer, a man writing, is the scribe of all nature; he is the corn and the grass and the atmosphere writing.

—HENRY DAVID THOREAU

July 2

Take notes on the spot: a note is worth a cart-load of recollections.

—RALPH WALDO EMERSON

July 3

Hartley fell down and hurt himself—I caught him up crying & screaming—& ran out of doors with him.—The Moon caught his eye—he ceased crying immediately—and his eyes & the tears in them, how they glittered in the Moonlight!

—SAMUEL TAYLOR COLERIDGE

July 4

What sort of diary should I like mine
to be? Something loose knit, & yet not
slovenly, so elastic that it will embrace
any thing, solemn, slight or beautiful
that comes into my mind.

—VIRGINIA WOOLF

July 5

When I write, I like to have an interval
before me when I am not likely to be
interrupted. For me, this usually means
the early morning, before others are
awake. I get pen and paper, take a glance
out of the window (often it is dark out
there), and wait. It is like fishing. But I
do not wait very long, for there is always
a nibble—and this is where receptivity
comes in. To get started I will accept
anything that occurs to me.

—WILLIAM STAFFORD

July 6

Sometimes what is written down is not generally understandable at all, but is a kind of private shorthand. The entry "6/8/92 woof!" records for me that on this day, and with this very doggy sound, I first came upon coyotes in the Provincelands.

—MARY OLIVER

July 7

The question then is not "What shall I write?" but rather, "Which, of the many beauties in my notebooks, do I want to carry forward?" The writer thus sits down to a feast every time, and never to an empty bowl.

—KIM STAFFORD

July 8

To get up in the cold, then make a warm place, have paper, pen, books to hand, look out at the gleaming rain, shadows, the streetlight steadfast. You could stay awake all night, not give away those hours.

—WILLIAM STAFFORD

July 9

Solitude gives birth to the original in us,
to beauty unfamiliar and perilous—and
to poetry.

—THOMAS MANN

July 10

I am so pulled hither and thither by circumstances. The calm, the coolness, the silent grass-growing mood in which a man *ought* always to compose,—that, I fear, can seldom be mine. Dollars damn me; and the malicious Devil is forever grinning in upon me. . . .

—HERMAN MELVILLE
to his friend Nathaniel Hawthorne

July 11

I believe that poems are made of words
and the breathing between them: that *is*
the medium.

—ADRIENNE RICH

July 12

Words exist because of meaning. Once you've gotten the meaning you can forget the words. Where can I find a man who has forgotten words so I can talk with him?

—CHUANG-TZU

July 13

The one thread I feel coming over and over in my life is the battle to preserve my perceptions, the battle to win through and to keep them—pleasant or unpleasant, painful or whatever . . . and how much they were denied.

—ADRIENNE RICH

July 14

When she turned fifty, her writing turned a corner. "You get older and braver," she said, "braver about what you can say and what can be understood."

—ELEANOR WACHTEL

on Carol Shields

July 15

"Did you make that song up?"
"Well, I sort of made it up," said Pooh.
"It isn't Brain . . . but it comes to me
sometimes."
"Ah," said Rabbit, who never let things
come to him, but always went and
fetched them.

—A.A. MILNE

July 16

I found the poems in the fields
And only wrote them down.

—JOHN CLARE

July 17

Originality depends on the faculty of noticing. Strange things happen in us and things not so strange. Cultivate the faculty of noticing or you will notice only what has been noticed and called to your attention before.

—ROBERT FROST

July 18

The length of his walk uniformly made the length of his writing. If shut up in the house he did not write at all.

—RALPH WALDO EMERSON
of Henry David Thoreau

July 19

Nothing seen, nothing said.

—THEODORE ROETHKE

July 20

The color of green and gray are what
bind me to the will to write poems.

—TESS GALLAGHER

July 21

The ideal life for a poet is to contemplate the word "is."

—CZESLAW MILOSZ

July 22

Writing is not only a technical process; it is also a joyous physical experience.

—ROLAND BARTHES

July 23

To watch someone writing big characters
a foot high. Ah, is this not happiness?

—CHIN SHENGT'AN

July 24

I am very cold without fire or covering.
. . . The robin is singing gloriously, but
though its red breast is beautiful, I am
all alone. Oh God, be gracious to my
soul and grant me a better handwriting.

—ANONYMOUS IRISH MONK

July 25

That absorbed, drudging, puzzled, sometimes inspired creature, herself, who sits at a desk trying to put words together.

—ADRIENNE RICH

July 26

I have a basic indolence about me which is essential to writing. It really is. Kids now call it space around you. It's thinking time, it's hanging out time, it's daydreaming time. You know, it's lie-around-the-bed time, it's sitting-like-a-dope-in-your-chair time. And that seems to me essential to my work.

—GRACE PALEY

July 27

Writing must be done in small amounts. I draft passages in notebooks, revise them, and make the final drafts on the typewriter. My speed is about a paragraph a day.

—GUY DAVENPORT

July 28

Creative work needs solitude. It needs
concentration, without interruptions. It
needs the whole sky to fly in, and no eye
watching till it comes to that certainty
which it aspires to. . . . Privacy, then. A
place apart—to pace, to chew pencils, to
scribble and erase and scribble again.

—MARY OLIVER

July 29

A writer is someone for whom writing is more difficult than it is for other people.

—THOMAS MANN

July 30

Outstanding events!—work and more work! The most outstanding seems to me the buying of an old caravan trailer which I had towed to out-of-the-way corners and where I sat self-contained with dogs, monk and work . . . writing in the long dark evenings after painting—loving everything terrifically. In later years my work had some praise and some successes, but the outstanding event to me was the doing which I am still at.

—EMILY CARR

July 31

I always kept writing uppermost. In the middle of the night, or even on a train, or going to class . . . If you really want to write something, you're not tired. You know, you can do anything you want to do . . . You have all the time in the world.

—MARK VAN DOREN

August

August 1

When you are lost, go deeper into the woods.

—MAIA

No man will ever unfold the capacities
of his intellect who does not at least
checker his life with solitude.

—THOMAS DE QUINCEY

You don't need to leave your room. Remain sitting at your table and listen. Don't even listen, simply wait. Don't even wait, be quite still and solitary. The world will freely offer itself to you to be unmasked. It has no choice. It will roll in ecstasy at your feet.

—FRANZ KAFKA

August 4

These leisurely, apparently aimless, ways of knowing and experiencing are just as "intelligent" as the other, faster ones. Allowing the mind to meander is not a luxury that can be safely cut back as life or work gets more demanding.

—GUY CLAXTON

What I see in America today is an almost religious zeal for the technological approach to every facet of life. It's a value system, a way of thinking, and it can become delusional.

—DANIEL YANKELOVICH

August 6

To do two things at once is to do neither.

—PUBLIUS SYRUS

August 7

The painter and the dancer, the actor
and the forger of swords, the potter and
the storyteller, the master in the art of
tea, and the master of the bow—even
the business person and statesman—all
prepare themselves for creative work
and decisions by sitting motionless and
practicing breathing.

—KARLFRIED DÜRCKHEIM

August 8

It is indeed in a state of emptiness and
tranquility that most ideas are conceived.

—LI JIH-HUA

August 9

I think I am probably in love with silence, that other world. And that I write, in some way, to negotiate seriously with it.

—JORIE GRAHAM

August 10

I've long believed that silence must be one of the poet's closest friends. If I were not able to enter the silence before words, how could I find any words I don't already know yet?

—JANE HIRSHFIELD

August 11

If you become still, help is already at hand.

—JOHANN WOLFGANG VON GOETHE

August 12

I think and think and think, I've thought myself out of happiness one million times, but never once into it.

—JONATHAN SAFRAN FOER

August 13

Everywhere in the world, when a stranger enters his house for the first time, the peasant submits him to the test of tranquility. . . . With his head slightly turned to one side, he listens to the silence emanating from the stranger's individual aura, which has an eloquence of its own, a series of noiseless vibrations that every human being evokes, quite apart from actions or words.

—KARLFRIED DÜRCKHEIM

August 14

When two people are conversing with
one another, a third is always present:
Silence is listening.

—MAX PICARD

August 15

It is a mistake, this extreme precision, this orderly and military progress; a convenience, a lie. There is always deep below it, even when we arrive punctually at the appointed time with our white waistcoats and polite formalities, a rushing stream of broken dreams, nursery rhymes, street cries, half-finished sentences and sights—elm trees, willow trees, gardeners sweeping, women writing—that rise and sink . . . .

—VIRGINIA WOOLF

August 16

Only by going alone in silence, without baggage, can one truly get into the heart of the wilderness. All other travel is mere dust and hotels and baggage and chatter.

—JOHN MUIR

August 17

May my silences become more accurate.

—THEODORE ROETHKE

August 18

We can make our minds so like still
water that beings gather about us that
they may see, it may be, their own
images, and so live for a moment with
a clearer, perhaps even a fiercer life
because of our quiet.

—W.B. YEATS

August 19

I remember once I just took everything
out of my life as much as I could, and
then started to put back in what I really
needed.

—PARKER HUBER

Kokoro is the Japanese word for heart. But it's not simply heart as the seat of the emotions; *kokoro* is also the seat of the intellect—the mind/heart, if you will. Thus the Sino-Japanese character for "idea" combines the ideograph for the word "sound" with the ideograph for *kokoro*. So an idea is a sound from the heart.

—KATHERINE PATERSON

August 21

Wherever we are, what we hear is mostly noise. When we ignore it, it disturbs us. When we listen to it, we find it fascinating.

—JOHN CAGE

August 22

One should listen to the sounds of birds in spring, to the sounds of cicadas in summer, to the sounds of insects in autumn, and to the sounds of snowfall in winter.

—LIN YUTANG

In the act of writing the poem, I am obedient, and submissive. Insofar as one can, I put aside ego and vanity, and even intention. I listen. What I hear is almost a voice, almost a language. It is a second ocean, rising, singing into one's ear, or deep inside the ears, whispering in the recesses where one is less oneself than a part of some single indivisible community. Blake spoke of taking dictation. I am no Blake, yet I know the nature of what he meant.

—MARY OLIVER

August 24

I don't know anything about
consciousness. I just try to teach my
students to hear the birds sing.

—SHUNRYU SUZUKI

August 25

If you want to know the truth of the matter, the music I prefer, even to my own or anybody else's, is what we are hearing when we are just quiet.

—JOHN CAGE

August 26

Imagination comes into us before it comes out of us. It is a receptive, a feminine process . . . imagination for me requires slowness; *slow and savor.*

—PAULUS BERENSOHN

August 27

To give your sheep or cow a large, spacious meadow is the way to control him . . . . It's the same with various images you have in your mind. Let them come and let them go.

—SHUNRYU SUZUKI

The Japanese school of Sumi painting
says, "If you depict a bird, give it space
to fly."

—PADMA HEJMADI

August 29

Today I'm going to lecture on confusion.
I'm all for it.

—THEODORE ROETHKE

That was a good day, in which each touch led to the next. Mistakes were as important as successes. Most of the time I didn't know where I was going, it was always potentially a really bad day.

—ANDY GOLDSWORTHY

August 31

Walking, I am listening to a deeper way. Suddenly all my ancestors are behind me. Be still, they say. Watch and listen. You are the result of the love of thousands.

—LINDA HOGAN

September

September 1

The spirit, by its very nature, is Slow.

—CARL HONORÉ

September 2

The transition from tenseness, self-responsibility, and worry, to equanimity, receptivity, and peace, is the most wonderful of all those shiftings of inner equilibrium . . . and the chief wonder of it is that it so often comes about, not by doing, but by simply relaxing and throwing the burden down.

—WILLIAM JAMES

September 3

When things happen too fast nobody
can be certain about anything . . . not
even about himself.

—MILAN KUNDERA

September 4

One of the shining moments of my day is
that when, having returned a little weary
from an afternoon walk, I exchange
boots for slippers, out-of-doors coat for
easy, familiar, shabby jacket, and, in my
deep, soft-elbowed chair, await the tea-
tray. Perhaps it is while drinking tea that
I most of all enjoy the sense of leisure.

—GEORGE GISSING

September 5

It is a transformative experience simply to pause instead of immediately filling up space.

—PEMA CHÖDRÖN

September 6

I refreshed myself by sitting on a wooden bench. I had no book to read, I took this opportunity to meditate briefly. The object I chose for meditation was a bush covered with roses. . . . It was filled, it was dense, it was choked with tiny dark garnet roses and fresh healthy leaves. So for the moment, I thought "rose"—"rose" and nothing else. I visualized the twigs, the roots, the harsh fuzz of the new growth hardening into spikes, plus all the botany I could remember . . . .

—SAUL BELLOW

September 7

The Present is the point at which time touches eternity.

—C.S. LEWIS

September 8

We have no letter from the world of emptiness, but when you see the plum flower, when you hear the sound of bamboo when hit by a small stone, that is a letter from the world of emptiness.

—SHUNRYU SUZUKI

September 9

I avoid looking forward and backward,
and try to keep looking upward.

—CHARLOTTE BRONTË

September 10

Please enjoy your spiritual childhood
here and now. Make it a cozy time you
can come back to in the future. We grow
older, and one day we will die. Take care
of the joyful present so that it can be the
joyful past.

—THICH NHAT HANH

September 11

Not all of us can do great things. But we can do small things with great love.

—MOTHER TERESA

September 12

Let me seek then, the gift of silence, and poverty and solitude, where everything I touch is turned into prayer, where the sky is my prayer, the birds are my prayer, the wind in the trees is my prayer, for God is all in all.

—THOMAS MERTON

September 13

The eye through which I see God is the same eye through which God sees me.

—MEISTER ECKHART

September 14

When we remove the world from our shoulders, we notice it doesn't drop. If you let it, it supports itself.

—JOHN CAGE

September 15

Just to be is a blessing. Just to live is holy.

—RABBI ABRAHAM HESCHEL

Can one reach God by toil? He gives himself to the pure in heart. He asks nothing but attention.

—W.B. YEATS

September 17

Taking a hot seat in the heart of a lotus. . .

—THEODORE ROETHKE

To do nothing at all is the most difficult thing in the world, the most difficult and the most intellectual. . . . [The] contemplative life, the life that has for its aim not *doing* but *being*, . . . not *being* merely, but *becoming*—this is what the critical spirit can give us. The gods live thus.

—OSCAR WILDE

September 19

This whole world is yours, you know.
You can breathe it and think about it and
dream it after this wherever you go. It's
all right. Nobody cares.

—WILLIAM STAFFORD

September 20

There is no day without its moments of paradise.

—JORGE LUIS BORGES

September 21

As a culture we're conditioned to want
newness. . . . But by always looking for
the new we rob ourselves of a deepening
relationship to the old. The pleasure
keeps on growing. It begins to have a
history.

—ARTHUR STRIMLING

September 22

The seventh day is a *palace in time*. It is made of soul, of joy and reticence.

—ABRAHAM HESCHEL

September 23

Sunday deserves to be, not a No-day, but
a Yes-day.

—ALASTAIR REID

September 24

A wise old Japanese once remarked to me, "If something is to acquire religious significance, it need only be simple and capable of repetition."

—KARLFRIED DÜRCKHEIM

September 25

What is Above is Within,
for everything in Eternity is translucent.
The Circumference is Within.

—WILLIAM BLAKE

September 26

There is a certain fertile sadness which I would not avoid, but rather earnestly seek. . . . My life flows with a deeper current, no longer in a shallow and brawling stream.

—HENRY DAVID THOREAU

September 27

Time has its own topography, with all sorts of different terrain that is not marked on the maps of our calendars and schedule books. . . . When you're traveling the terrain of time, the shortest distance between two points may be a detour.

—MARJORIE KELLY

September 28

In the economy of the spirit, thrift is ruinous.

—PAUL VALÉRY

September 29

Long deep rhythms like the turning of the planets and the drift of the stars, the decay of matter, the old turtle-creep of continents around the globe. Evolution. Over which lie the adagio rhythms of history, the play of fire over burning sticks.

—GUY DAVENPORT

September 30

When you do the same thing for your whole life, the things that are inessential start falling away. . . . You just go through life and try to be as kind as possible.

—MEREDITH MONK

October

October 1

What if you slept? And what if, in your sleep, you dreamed? And what if, in your dream, you went to heaven and plucked a strange and beautiful flower? And what if, when you awoke, you had the flower in your hand? Ah, what then?

—SAMUEL TAYLOR COLERIDGE

October 2

We must face not only the simple
guiding images alive in our breasts, but
the long years we have neglected them.

—DAVID WHYTE

October 3

You tell me you have had many dreams
lately, but have been too busy with
your writing to pay attention to them.
You have got it the wrong way round.
Your writing can wait, but your dreams
cannot, because they come unsolicited
from within and point urgently the way
[that] you must go.

—CARL GUSTAV JUNG
speaking to Laurens van der Post

October 4

Sixty percent of Americans report changing their sleeping habits so they can watch television.

—BILL MCKIBBEN

October 5

All night thoughts, in my own experience anyway, come as sharply and clearly as the sound of a silver bell or gong. . . . It is almost as if I had been shot through space, from one world to another, and words are simple and few in my mind, saying what I am waiting to hear.

—M.F.K. FISHER

October 6

It is as if one has a storage room where you have information you can't reach when you're awake. . . . Something you heard, something you saw, something that happened to somebody. A smell. A color. A texture. And you grab it. And you store it. And you're not aware of it at all. . . . And that is what your dream is about. It's bringing back information to your conscious mind that has always been there . . . . it's yours.

—ISABEL ALLENDE

October 7

If you dream of an egg hanging at your
bed's Head by a string [it] signifies
finding hidden Treasure.

—SAMUEL TAYLOR COLERIDGE

October 8

No dreams, however absurd or
senseless, are wasted in the universe.

—BRUNO SCHULTZ

October 9

There were periods in my life when I couldn't remember a single dream. I went around embarrassed, trying to imagine what dreaming would be like. At other times I found myself every night with a different cast of characters dressed like guests at a funeral. More freaks packed in one dream than in all the sideshows of the world.

—CHARLES SIMIC

October 10

We know ourselves in this mad crowd,
and owe to dreams a kind of divination
and wisdom.

—RALPH WALDO EMERSON

October 11

I have learned that dreams are more accurately set down in drawings (with color pens if dreaming in color) than in words. I divide the page into three sections because dreams are often in three acts, and do have beginning-middle-end.

—MAXINE HONG KINGSTON

October 12

I must devote some one or more Days
exclusively to the Meditation on *Dreams*.
Days? Say rather Weeks!

—SAMUEL TAYLOR COLERIDGE

As I grow familiar with my dreams, I grow familiar with my inner world. Who lives in me? What inscapes are mine? . . . These are the animals and people, places and concerns, that want me to pay attention to them, to become friendly and familiar with them. They want to be known as a friend would.

—JAMES HILLMAN

October 14

I love to lie hard and alone, yea and without a woman by me: after the kingly manner: somewhat well and warm covered. I never have my bed warmed; but since I came to be an old man, if need require, I have clothes given me to warm my feet and my stomach. . . . Sleeping hath possessed a great part of my life: and as old as I am, I can sleep eight or nine hours together.

—MICHEL DE MONTAIGNE

October 15

Lying in bed would be an altogether
perfect and supreme experience if only
one had a colored pencil long enough to
draw on the ceiling.

—G.K. CHESTERTON

October 16

It was told me in a dream
That I should do this
And I would recover.

—ALGONQUIN HEALING SONG

"Dreams are like fairy stories," she said, "and fairy stories are like dreams. They are reflections of each other, and they heal the sleeping mind."

—TAHIR SHAH

October 18

Asking the right question of your dream can wake you up to what you haven't paid attention to, to what is new, what is fresh, and what is being brought into your life that you haven't quite lived before. Asking the right question is essential to understanding your dreams.

—EDITH SOLLWOLD

October 19

I can never decide whether my dreams
are the result of my thoughts, or my
thoughts the result of my dreams. . . .
But my dreams make conclusions for
me. They decide things finally. I dream a
decision.

—D.H. LAWRENCE

October 20

All good writing is a guided dream.

—JORGE LUIS BORGES

I will have to break down and confess
to you that Stuart Little appeared to me
in a dream, all complete, with his hat,
his cane, and his brisk manner. Since
he was the only fictional figure ever to
honor and disturb my sleep, I was deeply
touched, and felt that I was not free to
change him into a grasshopper or a
wallaby.

—E.B. WHITE

October 22

We work in the dark—we do what we can—we give what we have. Our doubt is our passion and our passion is our task. The rest is the madness of art.

—HENRY JAMES

October 23

Flaubert was at vast pains to acquire
a stock of precise information about
objects, persons, places, and periods
with which his work was concerned,
though we are to understand that he
often wrote his actual descriptions from
visions for which his mind had been
thus prepared.

—T. STURGE MOORE

October 24

With the poetic vision . . . joy comes,
something enters into you. . . . Such a
vision often forms slowly, piece by piece
as the parts of a scene slide onto the
stage; but often also it is sudden and
fugitive like the hallucinations of sleep.
Something passes before your eyes; then
you must throw yourself eagerly upon it.

—GUSTAVE FLAUBERT

October 25

I've dreamt in my life dreams that have stayed with me ever after, and changed my ideas: they've gone through and through me, like wine through water, and altered the colour of my mind.

—EMILY BRONTË

October 26

To ask of a dream, what does it mean,
is as misguided as to ask the same
question of a person or a poem, or of a
sunset.

—JAMES HILLMAN

October 27

When the state of dreaming has dawned,
Do not lie in ignorance like a corpse.
Enter the natural sphere of unwavering
attentiveness.
Recognize your dreams and transform
illusion into luminosity.
Do not sleep like an animal. Do the
practice which mixes sleep and reality.

—TIBETAN BUDDHIST PRAYER BEFORE SLEEP

October 28

The dreams are larger than I am. They explain me more than I can explain them.

—DAVID BLUM

We are such stuff
As dreams are made on; and our little life
Is rounded with a sleep.

—WILLIAM SHAKESPEARE

October 30

Once upon a time, I, Chuang-Tzu, dreamed I was a butterfly . . . . I was conscious only of following my fancies as a butterfly, and was unconscious of my individuality as a man. Suddenly, I awoke, and there I lay, myself again. Now I do not know whether I was then a man dreaming I was a butterfly, or whether I am now a butterfly dreaming I am a man.

—CHUANG-TZU

October 31

In art and dream may you proceed with
abandon. In life may you proceed with
balance and stealth.

—PATTI SMITH

November

November 1

The world is a better place for having its stories told.

—GRACE PALEY

November 2

Howard Norman tells us that in the Crees' Garden, the exchange of information is round, and that stories are round. Stories live in certain places; they gather at night and talk to one another. Every so often a story goes out and inhabits someone for a while. When a storyteller begins a story, it is not by saying, "I'm going to talk about moose." *About* removes him. He says, "I'll talk moose."

—KATHERINE MCNAMARA

The telling and the hearing of a story is not a simple act. The one who tells must reach down into deeper layers of the self, reviving old feelings, reviewing the past. . . . As it enters the memory of the listener, it is augmented by reflection, by other memories, and even the body hearing and responding in the moment of the telling. By such transmissions, consciousness is woven.

—SUSAN GRIFFIN

A story's like a song, you know. It's really worth the being in it again.

—ARTHUR STRIMLING

November 5

Eternity is in love with the productions of time.

—WILLIAM BLAKE

Our period is obsessed with the desire to forget, and it is to fulfill that desire that it gives over to the demon of speed; it picks up the pace to show us that it no longer wishes to be remembered, that it is tired of itself; that it wants to blow out the tiny troubling flame of memory.

—MILAN KUNDERA

November 7

I'm very fast. I mean, I'm a New Yorker.
I speak a mile a minute. I can think three
thoughts at the same time . . . and I like
it that way. I enjoy it.

—SARAH SCHULMAN

November 8

Everything is busy here. The mind is
busy. There is busyness all around . . . .
In Nepal if someone is visiting from
another country, immediately I will drop
what I'm doing and run there to see
them. "Oh, I'm so happy to see you."
Here, everyone is tired.

—PRAJWAL

quoted by Warren Lehrer & Judith Sloan

November 9

In stories told in small towns, the living
carry the dead with them, and many
times a day commemorate their passing.

—HOWARD MANSFIELD

November 10

Memory is a kind
of accomplishment,
a sort of renewal . . .

—WILLIAM CARLOS WILLIAMS

November 11

I have liked remembering almost as much as I've liked living.

—WILLIAM MAXWELL

November 12

Those who observe quickly and vividly hold us with the details they see. Their stories have a flow that carries the reader.

—ROGER DEAKIN

November 13

What would one give to have him in a box, and take him out to talk!

—JANE WELSH CARLYLE
of Thomas De Quincey

November 14

People didn't usually tell each other
things that were happening to them at
that moment. But if it had happened
years ago—no matter how awful it
was—you could tell it.

—THE WHEELWRIGHT

quoted by Ronald Blythe

November 15

Troubles past are good to tell.

—YIDDISH SAYING

November 16

The act of telling a story creates community and, at the same time, elicits more stories.

—SAM KEENE

November 17

In every refugee site I visited, people literally lined up, as if waiting for food, to tell me their stories. All that mattered was that I had time to listen.

—EVE ENSLER

November 18

Every night I come up to my room and I lie on my little bed, and I tell myself the story of my life—just in case someone should ever ask.

—IMMIGRANT WOMAN
quoted by Arthur Strimling

November 19

A tale is better than food.

—ROBIN FLOWER

November 20

I became fascinated with the idea of poems that fell out of the air—"found poems, told poems" —poems that grew out of conversation.

—VERANDAH PORCHE

November 21

There is no one story and one story only.

—ADRIENNE RICH

November 22

When a story is told for the second time,
it's fiction, no matter what.

—GRACE PALEY

November 23

Stories move in circles. . . . So it helps if you listen in circles. . . . And part of the finding is the getting lost. And when you're lost, you start to look around and to listen.

—DEENA METZGER

November 24

Imagination, inspiration and intuition
are all arts of the ear.

—PAULUS BERENSOHN

November 25

 The old storyteller sat up tall. He
touched a thumb to his own chest.
"It's in there waiting," he said.
"What is?"
"Your story."
"Waiting for what?"
Mrabet closed his eyes.
"It's waiting for you to close your eyes
and wake up."

—TAHIR SHAH

November 26

Boredom is the dream bird that hatches the egg of experience.

—WALTER BENJAMIN

November 27

The Berbers believe that when people are born, they are born with a story inside them, locked in their heart. It looks after them, protects them.

—TAHIR SHAH

Stories held in common make and remake the world we inhabit. . . . The story we agree to tell about what a child is or who the bad guys are or what a woman wants will shape our thinking and our actions, whether we call that story a myth or a movie or a speech in Congress.

—URSULA LE GUIN

November 29

The universe is made of stories, not of atoms.

—MURIEL RUKEYSER

"Remember only this one thing," said Badger. "The stories people tell have a way of taking care of them. If stories come to you, care for them. And learn to give them away where they are needed. Sometimes a person needs a story more than food to stay alive."

—BARRY LOPEZ

December

December 1

Once, a very long time ago, walking
down the street in a Polish village, I
grew thoughtful at the sight of ducks
splashing about in a miserable puddle.
I was struck because there was a lovely
stream flowing through an alder wood.
"Why don't they go over to the stream?"
I asked an old peasant sitting on a bench
in front of his hut. He answered, "Bah! If
they only knew!"

—CZESLAW MILOSZ

December 2

It is never too late to be what you might
have been.

—GEORGE ELIOT

Me, if I'm depressed, I go down to
the A&P and admire the lemons and
bananas, the meat and milk.

—THEODORE ROETHKE

December 4

A little can be a lot if it's enough.

—GRANDMA GILBERT

December 5

We don't have to wait for some grand utopian future. The future is an infinite succession of presents, and to live now as we think human beings should live, in defiance of all that is bad around us, is itself a marvelous victory.

—HOWARD ZINN

December 6

If fate throws a knife at you, you can
catch it either by the blade or the handle.

—PERSIAN SAYING

December 7

If you're feeling poor or miserable, give something away—time or money or material goods—and immediately you'll feel better.

—KATHY O'ROURKE

December 8

If you are generous to someone, you are in effect making him [or her] lucky. That is important. It is like inviting yourself into a community of good fortune.

—TWYLA THARP

December 9

I make myself rich by making my wants few.

—HENRY DAVID THOREAU

The human impulse to make and mend and improvise is very strong. And modern life completely denies it. So when I made my plate-drainer, *yeah!* I'm always making bits and pieces for the garden. And instead of thinking, what can I buy, it's *what can I make it out of? How can I do it?* Which is a great feeling.

—FIONA HOUSTON

December 11

Be grateful for your life, every detail of it, and your face will come to shine like the sun, and everyone who sees it will be made glad and peaceful.

—ANDREW HARVEY

December 12

I permitted myself everything except complaints.

—JOSEPH BRODSKY

December 13

As we grow older we wish more and more to be young again, to return to youth with the wisdom of age . . . . We characteristically ignore a much more feasible kind of chronological magic— making present time slow its pace.

—ROBERT GRUDIN

December 14

Fast learns, slow remembers. Fast
proposes, slow disposes. Fast is
discontinuous, slow is continuous. . . .
Fast gets all our attention, slow has all
the power.

—STEWART BRAND

December 15

And late in life I discovered
a quiet joy
like a serious disease that's discovered too late:

just a little time left for quiet joy.

—YEHUDA AMICHAI

My greatest happiness consists in doing nothing whatever that is calculated to obtain happiness . . . . Perfect joy is to be without joy.

—CHUANG-TZU

December 17

Even a fire kisses itself.

—THEODORE ROETHKE

December 18

From early adulthood, I have spent much
of my time living, mentally, in the future.
. . . The current temptation, now that
the future has arrived, is to begin living
in the past: to remember the good old
days when I thought so much about the
future. Enough already. I have to lose my
yen for then, suture the future, and at
long last put the pow! in now—to make
every day, that is, as delight-filled as
possible.

—JOSEPH EPSTEIN

December 19

Each thing in the world asks us, "What makes you think I'm not something you like?"

—JOHN CAGE

December 20

I have often noticed that the things I have done with a happy heart, and with no inner repugnance, have a habit of succeeding happily, even during games of chance, where only fortune rules.

—RENÉ DESCARTES

December 21

Whenever I open a gap between myself and my screens, good things happen.

—WILLIAM POWERS

December 22

Renounce and enjoy.

—MOHANDAS GANDHI

December 23

Instead of consuming music, I'll make
music. Instead of consuming poetry,
I'll make poetry. Instead of consuming
food, I'll grow food. Every time you say
no to being a consumer and yes to being
a creator, you create a new world.

—ANDREW KIMBRELL

December 24

Art has something to do with the achievement of stillness in the midst of chaos. . . . an arrest of attention in the midst of distraction.

—SAUL BELLOW

December 25

I'm often asked, "Where do you get your ideas?" The short answer is: everywhere. It's like asking, "Where do you find the air you breathe?"

—TWYLA THARP

December 26

Every life has the same potential for depth and richness and integrity. But that potential is lost when your days are spread so thin that busyness is your true occupation.

—WILLIAM JAMES

December 27

Common sense and a sense of humor are the same thing moving at different speeds. A sense of humor is just common sense dancing.

—WILLIAM JAMES

December 28

A poet needs a library, a comfortable chair, a room to sleep in, hot water for a bath, and perhaps some trees outside the window. Nothing more.

—ZBIGNIEW HERBERT

December 29

He who knows that enough is enough
will always have enough.

—LAO TZU

December 30

I don't want anything in the world—I just like existing every minute and watching things coming and things going, and then coming again, like storms and sunshine and then storms again. I don't want anything at all for the simple reason that I have everything, or rather, which is the same thing, everything has me.

—WINIFRED NICHOLSON

December 31

The soul has its own sense of time, and
its own odd forms of clock and calendar.
Some days are long, some short.

—STEPHAN RECHTSCHAFFEN

Acknowledgements

Thanks so much to Laetitia Bermejo for the gorgeous illustrations, and to all at Bauhan Publishing for their dedication to beautiful and useful books, in particular to Henry James, Sarah Bauhan, Mary Ann Faughnan, Nerissa Osborne and Brie Morrissey. Thanks too to the many readers who have welcomed and cherished *World Enough & Time*, especially Eleanor Adams, Paulus Berensohn, Maddie Cahill, Penny Gill, Joy Holland, Phil Innes, Mariel Kinsey, E.B. Lehman, Gary Lenhart, Jehanne Marchesi, Gary Margolis, Daisy Mathias, Cathy O'Keefe, Holly Wren Spaulding, Arthur Strimling, Davis Te Selle & Paul Wapner.

World Enough & Time: On Creativity and Slowing Down

"The human mind," writes Christian McEwen, is "fed and nourished by every sight and smell and sound that we encounter, from the movement of the clouds to the shrill of the birds outside our morning window." To enjoy that nourishment, we need to "refuse and choose," resisting the siren call of technology whenever possible and allowing ourselves time to slow down and pay attention.

"*World Enough & Time* is a wise book—a quiet feast, a daydreamer's manual, a work of mindfulness, which teaches us to slow down and see the world anew. Read it slowly, and come to your senses."

—EDWARD HIRSCH

author of *How to Read a Poem and Fall in Love with Poetry*

ISBN: 978-087233-146-4, 368 pages, $22.95
www.bauhanpublishing.com/world-enough-and-time/

Christian McEwen is a freelance writer, teacher, and workshop leader. She has edited four anthologies, including *Jo's Girls: Tomboy Tales of High Adventure*, and *The Alphabet of the Trees: A Guide to Nature Writing*. She has written for the *Nation* and the *Village Voice*, her poems and essays have been widely published, and she helped produce the documentary film *Tomboys!* McEwen has taught poetry, creative writing, and environmental literature at a number of venues including the Scottish Poetry Library in Edinburgh, Williams College and Lesley University in Massachusetts, and the New School in New York. She has been a fellow at the Yaddo and MacDowell colonies. Born in London, McEwen grew up in the Borders of Scotland and currently lives in Northampton, Massachusetts.

WWW.CHRISTIANMCEWEN.COM

For many years, **Laetitia Bermejo** has painted the wild and willing figures she met and knew in many places around the world. She trained, swam and flew, bringing her pen and blank book along. She sat and walked and drew, her life as a  poem with her paintings as her song. Born in Leeds in England of French and Spanish parents, Bermejo received a Fine Arts degree at Slade School, University College, London. She lives in Mallorca.